Inventions from the Middle Ages

Chapter 5
Lesson 93: Other Suffixes: *-TION*, *-SION*, and *-OUS*
Lexile® Measure: 670L

Printed in the United States of America

Copyright © September 2012 by Reading Horizons

ISBN 978-1-62382-047-3

The period of time from 900 A.D. to 1200 A.D. is known as the Middle Ages. It was a tremendous time in history. This time period saw a continuous flow of new ideas. It also saw the production of many famous inventions.

Some of those inventions had their introduction during the Middle Ages. Of course, there have been revisions, but many of those inventions are still in use today. Since they are so numerous, we will mention only a few. Here is a description of four Middle Age inventions.

Wheelbarrow: a construction of a large wood or metal cart on wheels. It has long handles. Wheelbarrows were useful in the completion of many castles. They helped move stones from one location to another. A wheelbarrow required little exertion.

Eyeglasses: an invention to help people who have poor eyesight. In the 1200s, clear or glass stones were ground into a curved shape. They were put in metal frames to help people with their vision. Over time, there have been enormous improvements to eyeglasses. People using glasses in the Middle Ages did not have the option of various prescriptions and frames.

The Hourglass: a solution to help people tell time. During the late 900s, the hourglass was made. It was made from wood, metal, and blown glass bulbs. It was known as a "sand clock." The sand in the glass showed the number of minutes that had passed. The hourglass is still used all over the world for many different occasions.

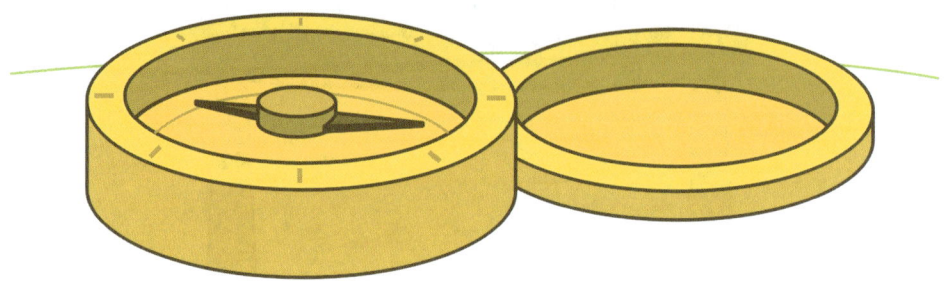

Compass: a device used to show direction. At first, compasses were invented and used by fortune tellers. They used a lodestone on a rock slab. With the addition of magnetized needles, compasses became common on ships. They helped with navigation. Without the compass, traveling on a ship could be very dangerous. Sailing in the wrong direction could create a hazardous situation.

Isn't this information fun? People who lived during the Middle Ages had a great passion for creating useful inventions. It is incredible that we still use these fabulous inventions!

The End

Comprehension Questions

1. The main idea of this passage is that inventions of the Middle Ages

    a. are still used today.

    b. are not in use today.

    c. don't exist anymore.

2. A wheelbarrow is

    a. a small wood or metal cart with large wheels.

    b. a large wood or metal cart on wheels, with long handles.

    c. a large wood or metal cart that needs to be plugged in to recharge.

3. Which of the following could be a new *invention* today?

    a. a television

    b. a flying chair

    c. a laptop computer

4. True or false: People in the Middle Ages used electricity to make their inventions.
   a. True
   b. False

5. Another name for the hourglass was
   a. a sand clock.
   b. a wristwatch.
   c. a grandfather clock.

Skill Words

addition	exertion	mention	revisions
completion	fabulous	navigation	solution
construction	famous	numerous	tremendous
continuous	hazardous	occasions	various
dangerous	information	option	vision
description	introduction	passion	
direction	inventions	prescriptions	
enormous	location	production	

Most Common Words

a	had	of	time
all	has	on	to
also	have	one	use
an	help	only	used
and	helped	or	useful
another	here	over	usng
are	ideas	people	very
as	in	put	was
at	into	saw	we
be	is	show	were
been	it	showed	who
but	known	so	will
by	large	some	with
could	little	still	without
did	lived	tell	world
different	long	that	
few	made	the	
first	many	their	
for	move	there	
four	new	these	
from	not	they	
great	number	this	

Challenge Words

period	poor	improvements	situation
course	eyesight	create	creating